LUNCH IN *Six*

30 easy vegetarian
and vegan lunch recipes

Never more than
6 ingredients

— *by* —

AND JANSEN SCHOUTEN

Table of Contents

Creamy Mushroom Penne	10
Celerybration Salad	12
Cranberry and Orange Sweet Potato Salad	14
Golden Leek and Pear Puff Pastry	16
Chickpea Tacos with Chargrilled Peppers	18
Avocado Chia Smoothie Bowl	20
Oven-baked Mega Mash	22
Sweet Roast Pumpkin with Rocket Pesto	24
Gnocchi Balboa	26
Saucy Oven Carrots with Smoky Tofu	28
Asian-style Hoisin and Ginger Spaghetti	30
Raunchy Sweet Potato Salad	32
Speedy Chickpea Stew	34
Ricotta and Mushroom Empanadas	36
Crispy Potato Medley	38
Royal Quesadillas	40
Crunchy Fennel and Grapefruit Salad	42
Melted Goat's Cheese with Honey and Pesto	44
¡Ay, caramba! Sweet Potato Salad	46
Italian Mozzarella Salad with Garlicky Croutons	48
Glass Noodles in Sweet Peanut Sauce	50
Have a Good Avo Cheddar Sandwich	52
Green n' Lean Power Salad	54
Cool Watermelon and Brash Bulgur	56
Crunchy Rostis with Green Asparagus	58
Moroccan Lentil and Feta Salad	60
Hawaii Toast	62
Chickpea Fritters with a Refreshing Cucumber Dip	64
Potato meets Beets	66
Luscious Fennel & Orange Polenta	68

Introduction

Hi! And welcome to *Lunch in Six,* the sequel to *Breakfast in Six.*

Much like Breakfast in Six, we created this book to help you, dear reader, eat as easily and tastily as possible.

Good food shouldn't be difficult to make, nor should it be heavily processed and highly-sugared to be delicious. Every recipe in this book is made with six or less ingredients — keeping it simple while introducing some incredible flavour combos.

Just like *Breakfast,* all of our recipes are vegetarian and many are vegan. Many more dairy and egg containing dishes can be made vegan and/or gluten-free. Look out for 'vegan options' and 'gluten-free options' on each recipe page. Jansen also includes his chef 'pro tips' to help you learn something new and practical for the kitchen.

Through personal experience we know exactly how difficult it can be to get a quick and tasty lunch — that's nutritious, too. So often we fall into the trap of grabbing lunch on the go (usually heavily processed and innutritious), going to a restaurant (expensive and often fattening) or skipping lunch entirely. We want to make lunch something to look forward to again.

Lunch in Six is our answer to the problem.

This is LUNCH IN Six

About HurryTheFoodUp

Otherwise known as Kat, Dave and Hauke, we have been sharing our passion (and recipes) for vegetarian food online since 2014. We firmly believe that the current food industry has gone insane, from awful and avoidable animal farming practices through to an extreme reliance on sugar-laden, heavily processed foods. This book is our answer to help anyone that wants it to take steps into a happier, healthier and more satisfying food life.

Jansen

To do this, we enlisted the help of Jansen, a good friend and incredible head chef hailing from the Netherlands, Europe. Jansen has cooked his way across the world, working in restaurants from New Zealand to Canada to Germany.

His wealth of experience is clear, and each recipe has been individually designed for either maximum taste from wonderful combinations of just six ingredients. As a family man, Jansen knows how tough ensuring everyone gets a good lunch can be — but his recipes show just how it can be done!

The Recipes

Throughout this book you will come across some of our absolute favourite food pairings — in all shapes and sizes.

Many of these not only work for lunch — they are combinations you can use to spice up breakfast, dinner and your overall cooking knowledge, too.

HurryTheFoodUp strives to be a healthy food website, priding ourselves on providing nutritious meals that have many clear health benefits. The same goes for Lunch in Six and the other books in the series, and most recipes included are indeed healthy and nutritious. We have also included a couple of 'naughty' recipes — after all, in moderation, we all deserve a little treat from time to time, right?

Every single recipe in this book is vegetarian and fourteen are vegan, with another eight that can easily be made vegan. Unfortunately the food world has many hidden animal products in it, which we will explain in just a moment.

The Ingredients

As mentioned, each recipe uses six or less ingredients.

We know that most people have access to a basic kitchen range, so, for clarity's sake, we have chosen several ingredients that we recommend always having a good stock of. These ingredients are not counted in the six ingredients or less section, and they are: salt and pepper, sugar, olive oil, butter, vinegar and balsamic vinegar. Each one is integral to many recipes — breakfast, lunch and dinner.

Salt   Pepper   Sugar   Olive Oil   Butter   Balsamic Vinegar   Vinegar

Vegetarian Animal Products

One item that often comes as a shock to people is non-vegetarian cheese. Many cheeses are sadly made with rennet, the juice taken from a baby calf's stomach. Cheeses made this way are naturally not considered as vegetarian, as they include the death of animal to produce them.

We highly recommend checking the packaging of cheese (or asking at the cheese counter) before you buy to see if they include animal rennet. Happily, more and more cheese producers are using non-animal rennet alternatives, so there is a good chance you can still get the variety of cheese you want in a vegetarian way.

It is also worth paying attention to foods that might include these cheeses — pesto, for example. Pesto is usually made with parmesan, a prime user of animal rennet. Again, check whether the jar states if it is vegetarian or not. If it doesn't say, it probably isn't.

Gluten-free

There are gluten-free varieties available of virtually any bread nowadays, if you look in the right stores. If gluten is an issue for you, please don't feel excluded from recipes that use bread — just check your local area for gluten-free alternatives.

THE
Recipes

Creamy Mushroom Penne

Vegan | Gluten-free Option

Servings: 2 | **Total Time:** 20 minutes
Best eaten: right away

Nutrition per serving:	**KCAL**	**FAT**	**CARBS**	**PROTEIN**
	543	27.5g	61g	17.5g

Ingredients

- 1 ½ cups penne pasta (1 ½ = 160g)
- 8 medium mushrooms (about 200g)
- 4 cornichons
- 1 cup vegan cream (1 cup = 250ml)
- 2–3 tbsp mustard
- 2 cups rocket (that's arugula by another name)
- Salt and pepper to taste
- 2 tbsp olive oil

Instructions

1. Place a large pot on the stove and boil the **penne pasta** in **salted water** until al dente.
2. Slice the **mushrooms,** heat up a frying pan on high heat and fry them with **oil** until they're nicely browned. 3–4 minutes should do it. Season with **salt and pepper.** Chop up the **cornichons.**
3. Let the frying pan cool down a bit, add the **cream,** and let it boil to reduce the liquid a little.
4. Add the **mustard** and the chopped cornichons. Give it a quick taste test and add more mustard if desired.
5. Drain the pasta when it's ready.
6. Add some **rocket** to a bowl, then a little pasta. More rocket, then more pasta. Leave a small well in the centre and tip in the **sauce.** Yummy!

Make it gluten-free

Grab yourself some gluten-free pasta! There's are plenty of options available now — lentil pasta is excellent.

Jansen's pro tip

The mustard is a big source (or is that sauce?) of flavour here so do make sure you taste test and add more if needed! Regular cream also works if you can't find/don't want to use vegan cream.

Celerybration Salad

Vegetarian | Gluten-free

Servings: 1 | **Total Time:** 10 minutes
Best eaten: right away, packed for lunch

Nutrition per serving:	KCAL	FAT	CARBS	PROTEIN
	374	21g	34g	16g

Ingredients

3 sticks green celery
½ cup feta cheese (½ cup = 70g)
4 tbsp pomegranate seeds
1 large orange
1 cup baby spinach
1 tbsp sesame seeds
¼ tsp salt
¼ tsp pepper

Instructions

1. Wash the **celery.** Be sure to wash it well, there's usually hidden sand/dirt!
2. Cut the celery into long, thin strips and put it in a salad bowl.
3. Cut the **orange** into segments and add to the bowl.
4. Squeeze any extra juice into the bowl.
5. Crumble the **feta** and add it along with the **spinach** and **pomegranate seeds.**
6. Serve and sprinkle the **sesame seeds, salt** and **pepper** over the top. Done!

Jansen's pro tip

The easiest way to get pomegranate seeds out is by holding a halved pomegranate over a bowl and giving it a good smack with something heavy. A big wooden spoon or rolling pin is ideal.

Cranberry and Orange Sweet Potato Salad

Vegan | Gluten-free

Servings: 2 | **Total Time:** 15 minutes
Best eaten: right away, packed for lunch

Nutrition per serving:	KCAL	FAT	CARBS	PROTEIN
	252	14.5g	29.5g	4g

Ingredients

- 4 cups mild salad (like romesco)
- 3 tbsp dried cranberries
- 1 large orange, zested and segmented
- 3 tbsp mixed nuts
- 1 medium sweet potato
- 2 tbsp olive oil
- 1 tbsp balsamic vinegar (or apple vinegar if you have it)
- Salt and pepper to taste

Optional

- Serve with soy yogurt or creme fraiche (for non-vegans)

Instructions

1. Peel the **sweet potato** and cut into small cubes, fry for 6–8 minutes on medium heat with a little **olive oil** (leave on the skin if it looks good, just give a quick clean).
2. Shred the **salad** in the meantime and put in large bowl. Give it a quick rinse first if it needs it.
3. Grate the **zest** from the **orange** and add it to the salad. Cut the **flesh** of the orange into pieces and add that as well. Throw in any juice that escapes.
4. Add the rest of the **olive oil** and **vinegar,** add **salt** and **pepper** to taste and give it a good mix. Add the sweet potatoes, put it on a plate and sprinkle the **mixed nuts** and **cranberries** on top. Enjoy!

Jansen's pro tip

Apple vinegar is great here! If you don't have it then balsamic or malt vinegar are more than fine alternatives.

14

Golden Leek and Pear Puff Pastry

Vegetarian | Gluten-free Option

Servings: 8 slices | **Total Time:** 30 minutes
Best eaten: right away

Nutrition per serving:	KCAL	FAT	CARBS	PROTEIN
	300	19g	20g	7g

Ingredients

1 piece of puff pastry, roughly 20×40cm
1 leek
1 fresh pear
4oz camembert or brie (4oz = 120g)
2 tbsp honey
4 tbsp walnuts
Pinch of salt

Instructions

1. Heat up the oven to 180°C/360°F.
2. Roll out the **puff pastry,** make sure the edges are slightly folded together so the cheese doesn't run out.
3. Slice the **pears** and **leek.** Roughly chop the **walnuts** and **cheese.**
4. Add the pears followed by the cheese, then the leek and top with walnuts.
5. Bake in the oven for 20 to 25 minutes until golden brown.
6. Sprinkle a little **salt** then drizzle **honey** over it. Enjoy!

Make it gluten-free

Gluten-free pastry is available from specialist shops — check out your local area!

Jansen's pro tip

I love to eat this as an 'open' pastry! You don't need to fold pastry over the top, simply layer the ingredients over the bottom and pop it in the oven!

Chickpea Tacos with Chargrilled Peppers

Vegetarian | Vegan Option | Gluten-free Option

Servings: 4 (2 tacos each) | **Total Time:** 15 minutes
Best eaten: right away

Nutrition per serving:	KCAL	FAT	CARBS	PROTEIN
	542	33g	56g	10g

Ingredients

8 taco shells
2 red bell peppers or 4 small, long red peppers (Cubanelle peppers)
1 can chickpeas (1 can = dry weight ca. 9oz/265g)
1 ripe avocado
1 cup sour cream (1 cup = 250ml)
2 tsp cumin
2 tbsp vinegar
1 tbsp olive oil
1 tsp salt
1 tsp pepper

Optional

A bunch of coriander, chopped. Some love it, some hate it. Your call! Add half to the sour cream and half to the chickpea mix.

Instructions

1. Heat up a grill pan, slice the **peppers** thinly and put a little **salt** and **olive oil** on them. Grill on high heat — both sides — until you have nice, thick black stripes. You can use a pan and fry if you don't have a grill.
2. Drain and rinse the **chickpeas.** Put in a bowl, add some **salt** and 2 tsp **cumin.**
3. Mash the **avocado** and add to the chickpeas, along with 1 tbsp of **vinegar.**
4. Add 1 tbsp of vinegar, and some salt and **pepper** to the sour cream.
5. Fill up the **tacos** with a bit of everything and enjoy!

Make it vegan

Use dairy-free sour cream — a soy version, for example.

Jansen's pro tip

Use corn tacos. They should naturally be gluten-free (but always check the labels!)

Avocado Chia Smoothie Bowl

Vegan | Gluten-free

Servings: 2 | **Total Time:** 3 minutes | **Best eaten:** right away

Nutrition per serving:	KCAL	FAT	CARBS	PROTEIN
	374	25g	39g	5g

Ingredients
- 1 avocado
- 2 small bananas
- 2 tbsp cranberries or raisins
- 2 tbsp hazelnuts
- 1 tbsp chia seeds
- 3 tbsp apple juice (or other fruit juice)

Instructions
1. Scoop out the flesh of the **avocado** and put in blender. Add the **bananas** and **apple juice.**
2. Blend until smooth (doesn't need much more than 30–60 secs in most blenders!).
3. Chop the **cranberries** and **hazelnuts.**
4. Serve the smoothie in a bowl with the chopped nuts and cranberries on top. Sprinkle the **chia seeds** on at the end. Done.
5. Enjoy!

Jansen's pro tip
I love serving and eating this one right away as it turns brown after a while and doesn't look quite so appealing!

Oven-baked Mega Mash

Vegan | Gluten-free

Servings: 2 | **Total Time:** 30 minutes
Best eaten: right away, packed for lunch

Nutrition per serving:	KCAL	FAT	CARBS	PROTEIN
	768	37.5g	101.5g	15g

Ingredients

- 3 large potatoes
- ⅔ cup almond milk (or cashew milk) (⅔ cup = 170ml)
- 2 tbsp roasted almonds
- 1 bunch parsley
- 10 sundried tomatoes (softened)
- 2 cups baby leaf salad (or any mild salad)
- 2 tbsp olive oil
- Salt to taste
- Pepper to taste

Instructions

1. Peel the **potatoes,** chop into rough pieces and boil in salty water (1 tsp salt should be fine) until they're soft.
2. In the meantime, chop the **parsley** and **sundried tomatoes.**
3. When the potatoes are ready, drain them and mash with a fork or masher, adding the **almond milk, sundried tomatoes, parsley** and **salt** and **pepper** to taste.
4. Put the mash into an ovenproof bowl (or bowls) and sprinkle some chopped **almonds** on top.
5. Bake them in the oven for about 10 minutes at 180°C/360°F.
6. While that's happening, prep the **baby leaf salad** with a simple dressing — **olive oil,** salt and pepper is great.
7. Serve all together. Done!

Jansen's pro tip

Any leftover sundried tomatoes, parsley and almonds are also a great add-on to the salad!

Sweet Roast Pumpkin with Rocket Pesto

Vegan | Gluten-free

Servings: 2 | **Total Time:** 30 minutes
Best eaten: right away, packed for lunch

Nutrition per serving:	KCAL	FAT	CARBS	PROTEIN
	772	45.5g	85g	16g

Ingredients

- ½ Hokkaido pumpkin
- ½ lemon, zested and juiced
- 1 apple
- ¾ cup quinoa (¾ cup = 125g/4oz)
- 2 cups rocket/arugula (2 cups = 150g/5oz) Rocket
- 3 tbsp pumpkin seeds (pre-bought to save time)
- 5 tbsp olive oil
- 1 ½ tsp salt
- 2 tbsp sugar

Jansen's pro tip

To cook quinoa, use double the amount of water to quinoa, add a little salt, and cook until the water has evaporated. Take it off the heat and cover with a tea towel for 5 mins. It should expand and go fluffy and light.

Instructions

1. Preheat the oven to 180°C/360°F.
2. Wash the **Hokkaido pumpkin,** scrape out the seeds and cut half of it in small cubes (1×1cm). You don't need to peel the skin.
3. Put the **pumpkin pieces** on an oven tray and sprinkle with **salt** and **olive oil.** Roast in the oven for 15–20 minutes — poke with a knife to check they're soft.
4. Cook the **quinoa** according to instructions on the package.
5. Cut the **apple** into small cubes.
6. Wash the **rocket** well and put **half of it** into the blender with 4 tbsp **oil,** 1 tsp of **salt, lemon juice** and **zest.**
7. In a small pan, heat up 2 tbsp of **sugar** on low-med heat — when it starts to brown toss in 3 tbsp of **pumpkin seeds** and let it caramelize for a couple of seconds. Let it cool, take the mix out of the pan then crush with a knife into pieces.
8. In a big bowl, toss the pumpkin, the quinoa, apple and the rest of the rocket together. Plate it and drizzle **rocket pesto** on top — finally add the caramelized pumpkin seeds.

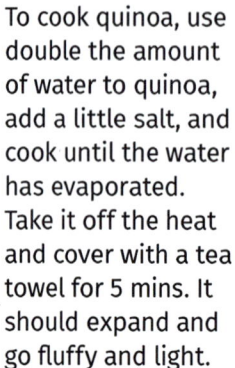

Gnocchi Balboa

Vegan | Gluten-free Option

Servings: 2 | **Total Time:** 20 minutes
Best eaten: right away, packed for lunch

Nutrition per serving:	KCAL	FAT	CARBS	PROTEIN
	711	36g	85g	15.5g

Ingredients

- 2 cups basil leaves
- 2 tbsp pine nuts
- 1 pack of your favourite gnocchi (14oz = 400g)
- 1 medium zucchini
- ½ red onion
- 1 clove of garlic
- 4 tbsp olive oil
- 1 ½ tsp salt
- ½ tsp pepper

Instructions

1. Bring a pan of salted **water** (add 1 tsp salt) to the boil.
2. Thinly slice the **zucchini** and **onion** and fry them on medium heat with 1 tbsp **olive oil** for 6–8 minutes, until soft.
3. Use a hand blender or food processor to blend the **basil** with 1 tbsp of **pine nuts**, 3 tbsp **olive oil**, ½ tsp **salt**, ½ tsp **pepper** and the **garlic**. Leave a few leaves of **basil** for garnishing later.
4. Boil the **gnocchi** according to package instructions and drain when finished.
5. When everything is cooked, mix the **zucchini-onion** with the gnocchi. Add to a bowl and drizzle the basil pesto on top. Garnish with more pine nuts and basil leaves. Done!

Make it gluten-free

Double-check your gnocchi to make sure they're gluten-free!

Jansen's pro tip

Although I am not a big fan of buying convenience food, I like to buy gnocchi every now and then. Sweet potato ones exist these days, too. They're a great staple to keep around the house, and if you buy ones without egg they last for ages!

Saucy Oven Carrots with Smoky Tofu

Vegan | Gluten-free

Servings: 2 | **Total Time:** 30 minutes
Best eaten: right away, packed for lunch

Nutrition per serving:	KCAL	FAT	CARBS	PROTEIN
	432	25g	37g	18g

Ingredients

- 4 carrots
- 5oz sugar snap peas (5oz = 150g)
- 1 cup smoked tofu (1 cup = 250g)
- 1 head romaine lettuce (or similar)
- 2 tbsp maple syrup
- 1 tbsp mustard
- 2 tbsp olive oil
- 1 tsp vinegar
- Salt to taste

Instructions

1. Preheat the oven to 170°C/340°F.
2. Wash the **sugar snaps** and **carrots.** Cut the carrots in half length-ways. Dice the **smoked tofu** in 1×1 cm cubes. Place these ingredients on a baking tray, drizzle 1 tbsp of **olive oil** and add a good pinch of **salt.** Make sure everything is nicely coated.
3. Roast for 20 minutes.
4. Wash the **lettuce** and shred.

For the dressing

1. Combine the **maple syrup** with the **mustard,** the rest of the **olive oil, vinegar** and a pinch of **salt.**
2. When ready, combine the roasted ingredients with the salad and dressing. Enjoy warm or cold!

Jansen's pro tip

Sugar snaps need a little less time to roast than the carrots. So, depending on your oven make sure to check back after 12–15 minutes and see if the snaps need to come out. If yes, take out the rest as well. A little crunch won't hurt the carrots one bit.

Asian-style Hoisin and Ginger Spaghetti

Vegan | Gluten-free Option

Servings: 2 | **Total Time:** 20 minutes
Best eaten: right away

Nutrition per serving:	KCAL	FAT	CARBS	PROTEIN
	580	23g	85.5g	18g

Ingredients

1 cup spaghetti (1 cup = 180g)
½ broccoli
1 spring onion
2 tsp ginger
4 tbsp hoisin sauce
3 tbsp sesame seeds (or black sesame seeds if you have them)
2 tbsp olive oil
½ cup water
Salt to taste

Instructions

1. Wash the **broccoli** and cut into little florets, thinly slice the **spring onion.**
2. Boil water and cook **spaghetti** according to package instructions.
3. In a big pan, fry the **broccoli** for 8 minutes on medium heat with some **oil** and the **water.** Grate the **ginger** and add it. If you have put a lid on top.

For the sauce

1. In a bowl mix together the **hoisin sauce, sesame seeds,** a pinch of **salt** and 4 tbsp of water.
2. When the spaghetti is cooked, drain it, and put it back into the pot. Now stir in the sauce and add the broccoli and spring onion.

The pasta dish needs to be nicely soaked in the sauce. If it's too dry add a bit of water, salt and/or hoisin sauce.

Enjoy immediately for best taste!

Make it gluten-free

To make it gluten-free rice or soba noodles are an excellent choice. As with all pastas, check the package first.

Jansen's pro tip

Still got that bottle of sesame oil that you used once laying around and forgot about? Now it's the time to use it again — fry the broccoli with sesame oil for an extra flavour kick!

Raunchy Sweet Potato Salad

Vegan | Gluten-free

Servings: 2 | **Total Time:** 30 minutes
Best eaten: right away, packed for lunch

Nutrition per serving:	KCAL	FAT	CARBS	PROTEIN
	663	35.5g	84.5g	15g

Ingredients

- 1 large sweet potato (ca. 14oz/400g)
- 1 ripe avocado
- 10 cherry tomatoes
- 2 tbsp cashew nuts
- 2 cups baby leaf (or your favourite mild salad)
- 1 lime, zest and juice
- 2 tbsp olive oil
- 1 tsp salt
- ½ tsp pepper

Instructions

1. Heat up the oven to 180°C/360°F.
2. Cut the **sweet potato** into small cubes. Toss them in a bowl with ½ tsp **salt** and some of the **olive oil,** place them on a tray and put in the oven for about 25 minutes, until they're soft.
3. Mash one half of the **avocado,** cut the other half into pieces. Cut the **cherry tomatoes** into quarters. Put it all in a bowl and add the **lime zest** and **juice** and **cashew nuts.**
4. Season with salt, **pepper** and a little more olive oil.
5. Let the sweet potato cool down a bit and add it to the bowl as well.
6. Add the **salad** and give it a good toss. Ready!

Jansen's pro tip

Bake the sweet potato the night before so you can take the salad with you to work. When it's cold, place it in a sealable lunch box or jar and add the lime juice, zest and olive oil. After that add the avocado, tomatoes — make sure they're covered in lime juice, too. Finally, add the nuts and salad. Seal and take!

Speedy Chickpea Stew

Vegan | Gluten-free Option

Servings: 2 | **Total Time:** 20 minutes
Best eaten: right away, packed for lunch

Nutrition per serving:	KCAL	FAT	CARBS	PROTEIN
	375	3.5g	74g	16g

Ingredients

1 can chickpeas
(1 can = 14oz/400g wet weight)
1 can chopped tomatoes
(1 can = 14oz/400g)
1 yellow bell pepper
1 tsp coriander powder
4 tbsp chopped parsley
1 tbsp sugar
2 slices of bread
Salt and pepper to taste

Optional
½ tsp cumin

Instructions

1. Heat up a pot and quickly roast the **coriander powder** with the **sugar** on a medium heat. This just needs 2–3 minutes.
2. Add the **tomatoes** and **chickpeas** to the pot.
3. Cut the ~~paprika~~ *pepper* into small cubes, and add it too.
4. Let it all simmer for 12–15 minutes, stirring occasionally.
5. Season with **salt, pepper** and **parsley.** Enjoy with some crusty **bread.**

Make it gluten-free

Bread can easily be left out for this recipe. Also, gluten-free bread is available in many places now — see if your local bakery has some!

Jansen's pro tip

We have an Indian restaurant around the corner where we sometimes order takeout. One of our favourites is their chickpea masala. It's fruity, spicy and a little sweet. The parsley freshens it up. If you have cumin laying around throw ½ tsp of that in, too. Really easy recipe but healthy, quick and vegan :)

Ricotta and Mushroom Empanadas

Vegetarian | Gluten-free Option

Servings: 6 empanadas | **Total Time:** 30 minutes
Best eaten: right away, packed for lunch

	KCAL	FAT	CARBS	PROTEIN
Nutrition per serving:	168	11.5g	13.5g	3g

Ingredients

- 1 piece of puff pastry, roughly 20×40cm
- 1 red bell pepper
- 2 tbsp ricotta
- 7 small mushrooms
- 1 tbsp fresh thyme
- 1 tsp harissa (or 1 tsp sambal oelek/sriracha)
- ½ tsp salt
- ½ tsp pepper
- 1 tbsp olive oil

Instructions

1. Preheat the oven to 200°C/390°F.
2. Chop the red **bell pepper** and **mushrooms** into small pieces. Fry with **olive oil** on medium heat for 2–3 minutes.
3. Add the chopped **thyme** at the end. Remove from heat and season with **salt, pepper** and **harissa**. Let it cool down a little bit and add the **ricotta**.
4. Roll out the **puff pastry** on parchment paper and cut six same-sized squares.
5. Put the **mixture** in, add a little bit of water to the edges of the **pastry** and fold it over into triangle shapes. Press the edges down gently.
6. Bake in the oven for 15–20 minutes (until it's crispy and brown). Done!

Make it gluten-free

Gluten-free pastry is now a thing — check your local specialist store!

Jansen's pro tip

Water works just as well as egg to for holding pastry together. Just press the edges down a little and you're set!

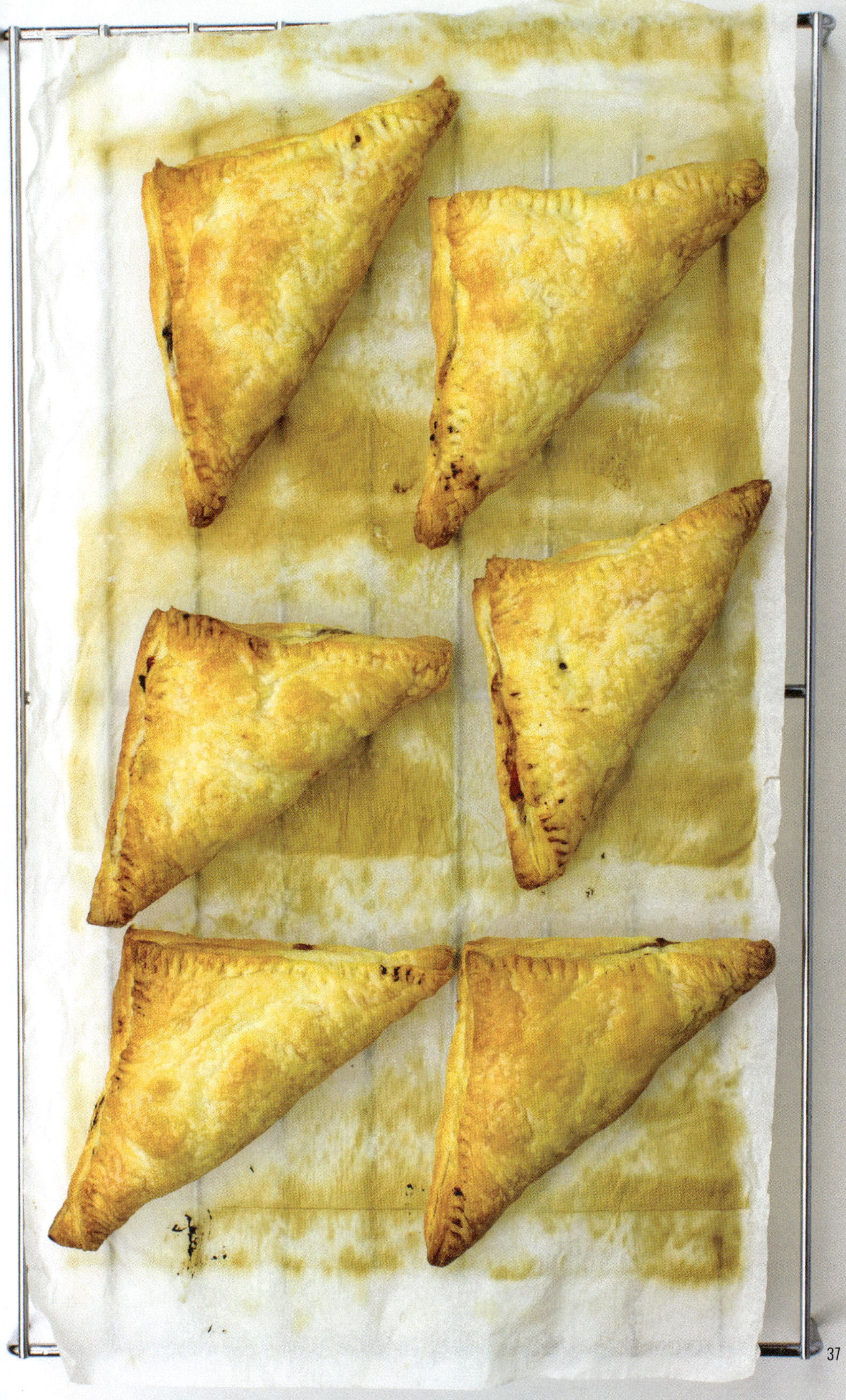

Crispy Potato Medley

Vegan | Gluten-free

Servings: 2 | **Total Time:** 30 minutes
Best eaten: right away

Nutrition per serving:	KCAL	FAT	CARBS	PROTEIN
	439	15g	70g	11.5g

Ingredients

- 8 small potatoes
- 2 cups spinach
- 1 small red onion
- 1 red bell pepper
- 1 medium zucchini *(courgette)*
- 10 medium brown mushrooms (about 250g)
- 3 tbsp olive oil
- 1 ½ tsp salt
- ½ tsp pepper

Instructions

1. Boil the **potatoes** in **salty water** (1 tsp **salt** should be fine) until soft. If the skin looks good, leave it on.

2. In the meantime, cut the **bell pepper, mushrooms** and **zucchini** into equal size small chunks.

3. Thinly slice the **red onion.** When the potatoes are soft (poke with a knife to check), drain them.

4. Heat up a big frying pan, cut the potatoes into quarters and fry them on medium heat until browned. When they're almost done, add the paprika/mushrooms/zucchini and fry it all together. Depending on the size you've cut the veggies, this will take about 5–6 minutes.

5. When everything is ready, throw in the raw **red onion** and the **spinach,** season with **salt** and **pepper** and enjoy.

Jansen's pro tip

Boil the potatoes the night before! Not only do they fry from cold really well, you'll make lunch super-quick! If you don't like raw red onion, throw it in when you fry the rest of the vegetables.

38

39

Royal Quesadillas

Vegetarian | Vegan Option | Gluten-free Option

Servings: 2 | **Total Time:** 25 minutes | **Best eaten:** right away

1. "Kat" Nutrition per serving:	KCAL	FAT	CARBS	PROTEIN
	618	31g	69g	21g

4 tortilla wraps
2 tomatoes
1 spring onion
⅓ cup sour cream (⅓ cup = 100g)
1 cup baby spinach (1 cup = 50g)
½ cup cheddar cheese, grated (½ cup = 60g)
Salt and pepper to taste

1. Slice the **tomatoes** and **spring onion**, season with **salt** and lots of **pepper**.
2. Spread out the **sour cream** on one half of the **tortilla**, layer the **tomatoes, spring onion, spinach** and **cheese** on top.
3. Fold the other half of the tortilla over.
4. Heat up pan and fry both sides on medium heat for 3–4 minutes. A big spatula is the easiest way to flip them.

2. "Sofia" Nutrition per serving:	KCAL	FAT	CARBS	PROTEIN
	655	31g	78g	22g

4 tortilla wraps
½ cup hummus (½ cup = 120g)
½ red onion
1 zucchini *Corgette*
½ red bell pepper
½ cup feta (½ cup = 75g)
1 tbsp olive oil
Salt and pepper to taste

1. Cut the **zucchini** into thin stripes and fry with some **oil** on high heat for a couple of minutes.
2. Cut the **red onion** and **paprika** into thin stripes. Crumble the **feta**.
3. Spread out the **hummus** on one half of the **tortilla**, put the **zucchini, red onion, paprika** and **feta** on top. Season with a little **salt** and **pepper**.
4. Fold the other half of the tortilla over.
5. Heat up pan and fry both sides on medium heat for 3–4 minutes. A big spatula is the easiest way to flip them.

Make it vegan
Use hummus instead of sour cream and vegan cheese instead of cheddar or feta!

Make it gluten-free
Be sure to use corn tortilla wraps! And always check the packaging.

41

Crunchy Fennel and Grapefruit Salad

Vegan | Gluten-free

Servings: 1 | **Total Time:** 10 minutes
Best eaten: right away, packed for lunch

Nutrition per serving:	KCAL	FAT	CARBS	PROTEIN
	340	19.5g	41.5g	7g

Ingredients

1 fennel
1 grapefruit
2 tbsp dried cranberries
2 cups baby spinach (2 cups = 100g)
½ red onion
2 tbsp olive oil
1 tsp sugar
Salt to taste

Instructions

1. Slice the **fennel** as thinly as you can — use a mandoline if you have one. Otherwise a good, sharp knife will do. Knead it with a spoon and a little **sugar** and **salt** and the fennel will become softer.
2. Zest quarter of the **grapefruit skin,** take out all the **segments** and use all the **juice.** Add it to the fennel.
3. Dice the **red onion,** add it and the **cranberries** to the fennel-mix.
4. Give it another pinch of **salt,** drizzle some **olive oil** on top and toss the **spinach** in it.
5. Make sure it's all mixed well, and serve!

Jansen's pro tip

You really have to slice the fennel as thinly as possible; if it's too thick it's not so nice to eat. Just watch your fingers!

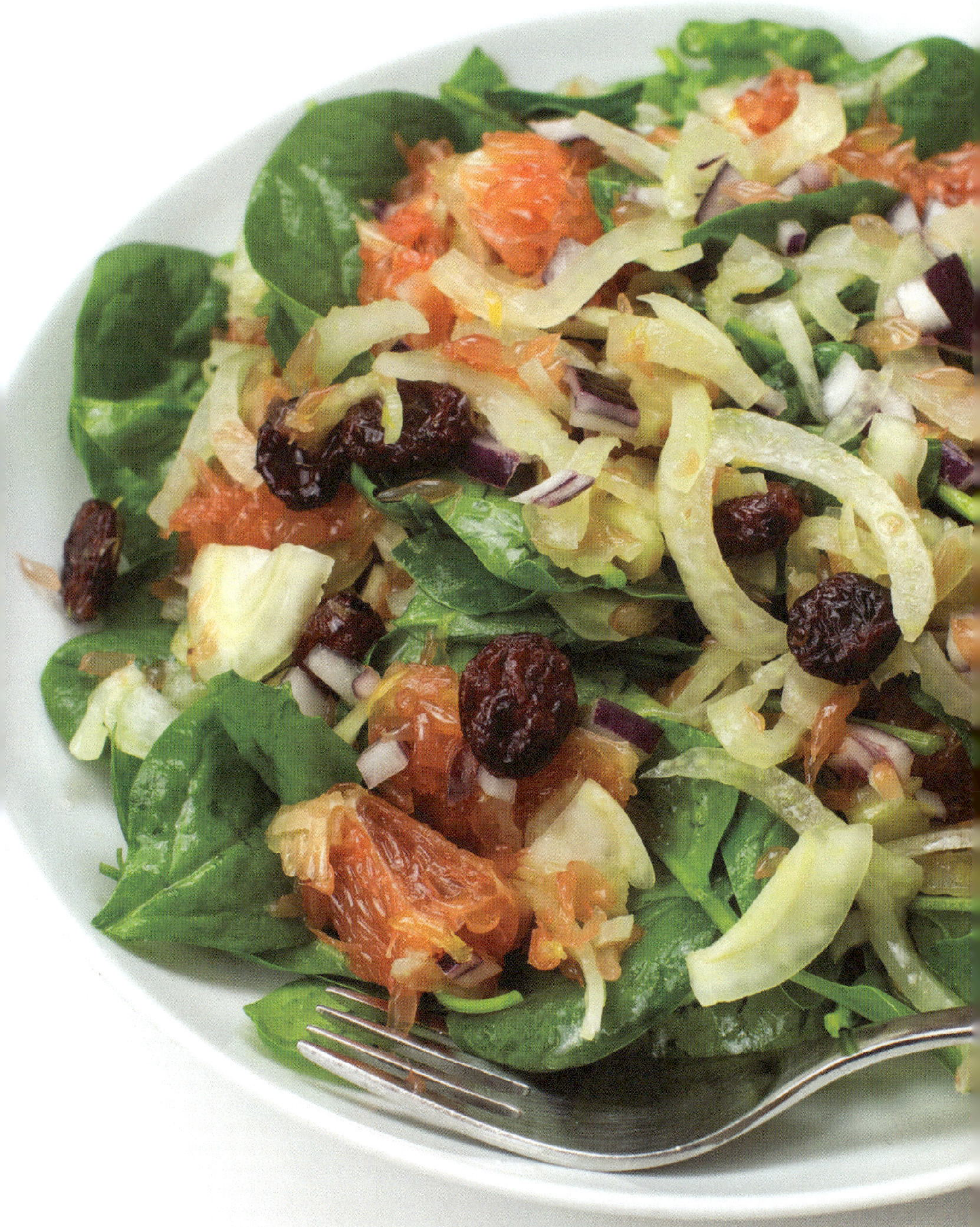

Melted Goat's Cheese with Honey and Pesto

Vegetarian | Gluten-free Option

Servings: 4 slices | **Total Time:** 10 minutes
Best eaten: right away

	KCAL	FAT	CARBS	PROTEIN
Nutrition per serving:	235	10.5g	29g	8.5g

Ingredients

- 4 slices of nice whole wheat or rye bread
- 2oz goat's cheese (2oz = 55g)
- 2 tbsp honey
- 1 handful of baby spinach
- 4 tbsp of your favourite pesto
- 1 fresh pear
- Salt to taste

Instructions

1. Thinly slice the **pear** and slice the **goat's cheese.**
2. Spread the **pesto** on each slice of **bread.**
3. Layer the **spinach** next, then pear, then the goats cheese on top. Drizzle a little **honey** next. Season with a pinch of **salt.**
4. Stick under the grill for 4–5 minutes. Done! If you're feeling naughty add a little more honey. Yummy.

Make it gluten-free

Lots of places do gluten-free bread now — see if your local bakery or supermarket does, too!

Jansen's pro tip

If you're not a fan of goat's cheese just replace it with your favourite. Most types fit really well!

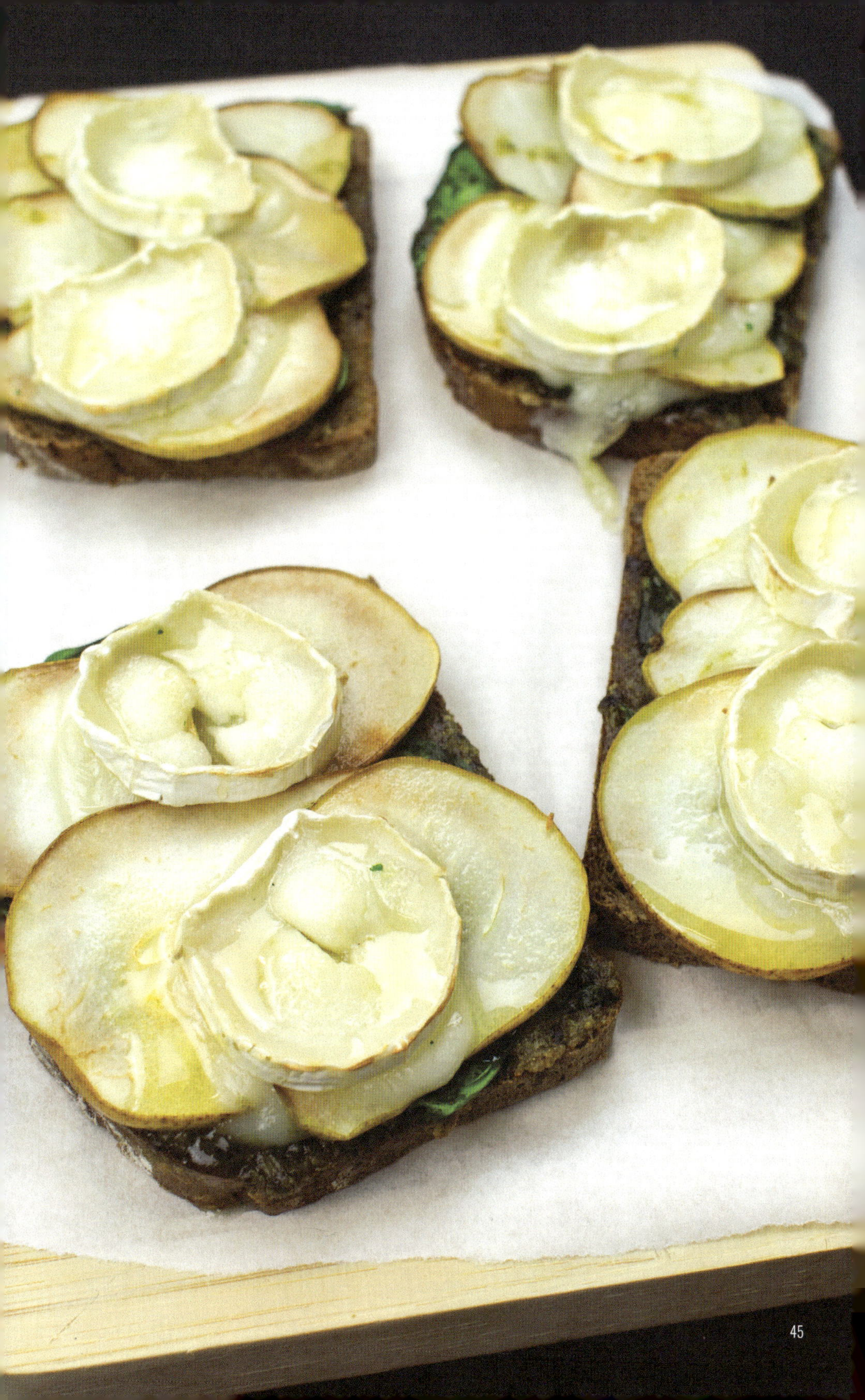

¡Ay, caramba! Sweet Potato Salad

Vegetarian | Vegan Option | Gluten-free Option

Servings: 2 | **Total Time:** 30 minutes
Best eaten: right away, packed for lunch

Nutrition per serving:	KCAL	FAT	CARBS	PROTEIN
	619	22g	93g	16.5g

Ingredients

- 1 large sweet potato (ca. 14oz/400g)
- ¾ cup couscous (¾ cup = 125g)
- 2 generous tbsp creme fraiche or soy yogurt
- 10 cherry tomatoes
- ¼ cucumber
- 1 tbsp cajun spice
- ½ tsp salt

Instructions

1. Heat up the oven to 180°C/360°F, cut the **sweet potato** in half (lengthwise) and sprinkle a little **salt** on it. Put it in the oven for 20–25 minutes, poke with a knife to check it's soft.

2. Cook the **couscous** according to the packet instructions and with the **cajun spice** and salt.

3. Cut the **cucumber** into small pieces, quarter the **cherry tomatoes** and add a little more salt to taste. Place in a bowl and add the cooked couscous.

4. Once the sweet potato is ready, scoop it out and place it on a plate. Cover it with the **couscous-mix** and add the **creme fraiche** or **soy yogurt** to serve.

Make it vegan

Just use a non-dairy yogurt (like soy) instead of creme fraiche!

Make it gluten-free

Couscous is full of gluten, and gluten-free couscous is hard to find, though not impossible. If you can't find any, you could use quinoa or brown rice instead.

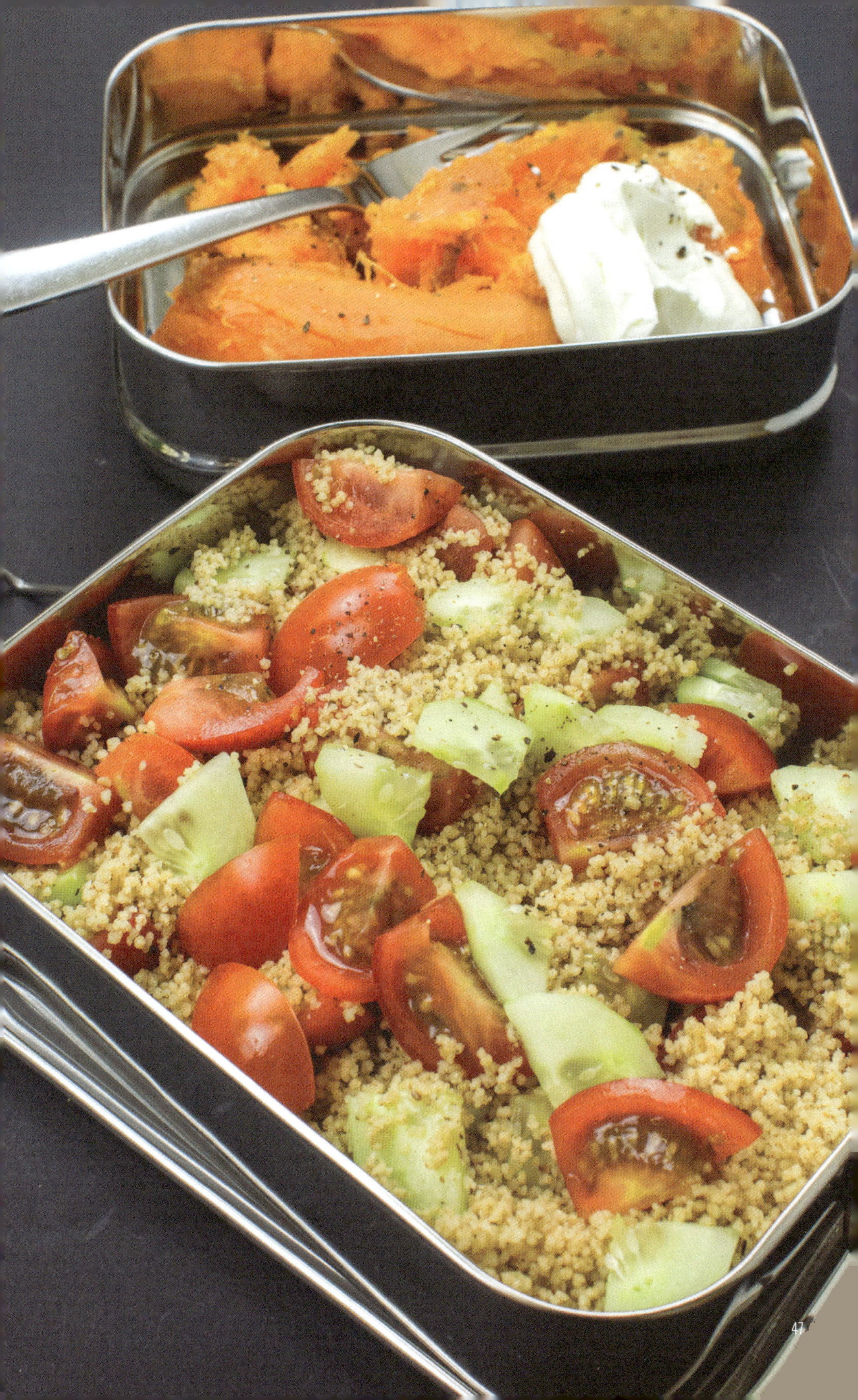

Italian Mozzarella Salad with Garlicky Croutons

Vegetarian | Gluten-free Option

Servings: 2 | **Total Time:** 10 minutes
Best eaten: right away

Nutrition per serving:	**KCAL**	**FAT**	**CARBS**	**PROTEIN**
	493	31g	40g	16g

Ingredients

- 1 bread roll from yesterday (slightly hardened is good :-))
- 3 large, ripe tomatoes
- 1 ball mozzarella (ca 125g/4.5oz)
- 10 basil leaves
- 2 cloves garlic
- 1 spring onion
- 3 tbsp olive oil
- Salt and pepper to taste

Instructions

1. Cut the **bread** into 1×1cm cubes. Heat up a frying pan at medium heat. Fry the bread in **olive oil** until golden brown. When it's almost done, throw in the **garlic** and fry for another minute.

2. Cut the **tomatoes** and **mozzarella** into pieces and thinly slice the **spring onion**. Chop or rip the **basil** leaves.

3. Put everything together in a bowl, give it a good toss, season with **salt, pepper** and olive oil.

Make it gluten-free

Simpy use gluten-free bread — available so widely now!

Jansen's pro tip

Really easy but very tasty — it's a great combination of flavours and a great way to use up old bread that's beginning to turn stale!

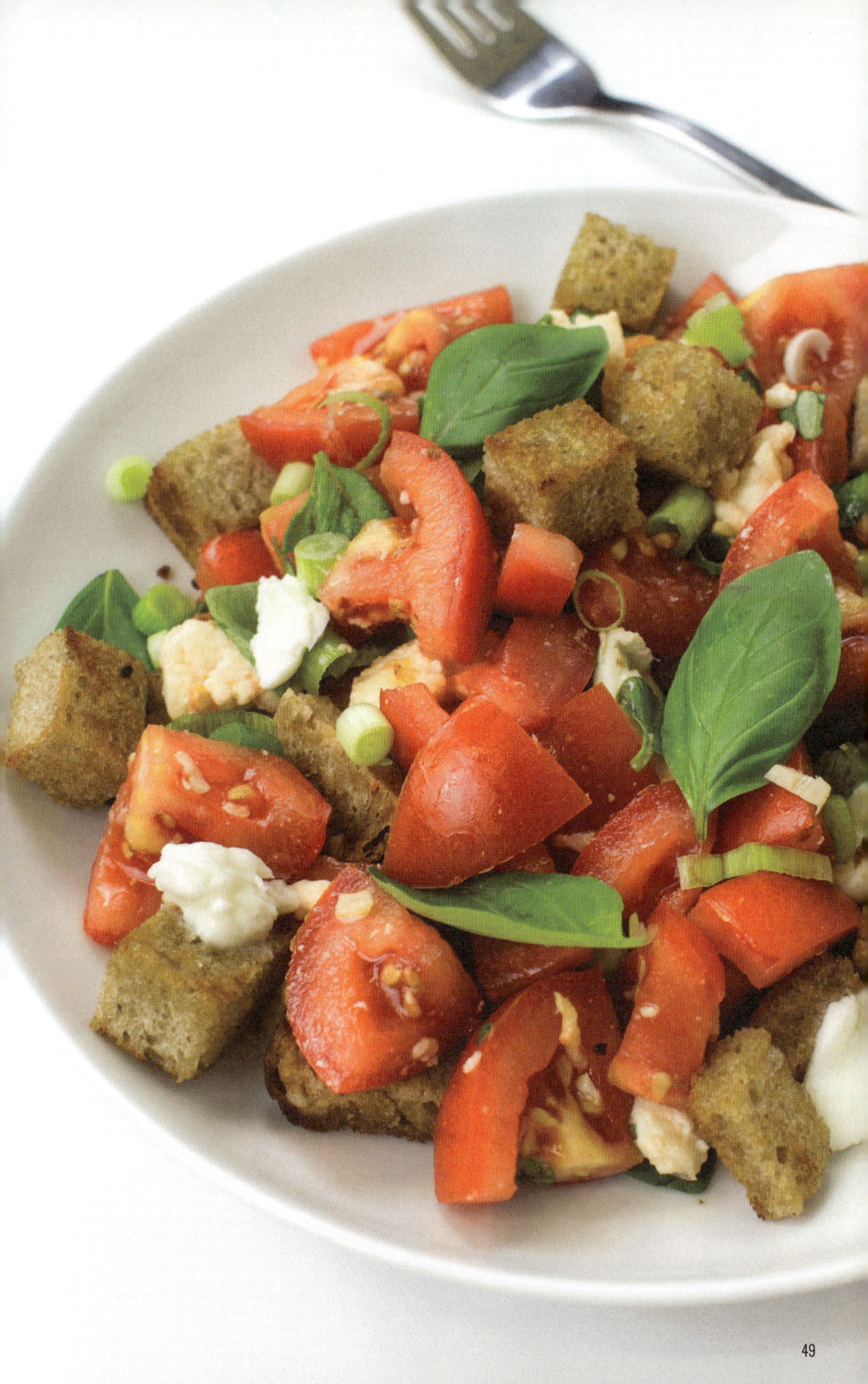

Glass Noodles in Sweet Peanut Sauce

Vegan | Gluten-free

Servings: 3 | **Total Time:** 10 minutes
Best eaten: right away, packed for lunch

Nutrition per serving:	KCAL	FAT	CARBS	PROTEIN
	413	8g	75g	12.5g

Ingredients

- 1 pack glass noodles (3.5oz/100g)
- 4 tbsp ketjap manis (if you can't find this, mix 3 tbsp soy sauce with 1 tbsp honey instead)
- 1 tbsp vinegar
- 2 tsp peanut butter
- 2 handfuls leafy salad
- 3 tbsp cashew nuts
- 5oz sugar snap peas (5oz = 150g)
- 1 tsp olive oil
- 1 tsp salt

Instructions

1. Cook the **glass noodles** as per packet instructions.
2. Mix together the **ketjap manis, vinegar, peanut butter** and a good pinch of **salt** in a bowl.
3. Add the cooked glass noodles to the bowl and give it a good mix.
4. Mix the **leafy salad** and **cashew nuts** too.
5. Fry the **sugar snaps** with **olive oil** for 2 minutes in a frying pan on medium heat. Don't overcook, we want them crispy and green.
6. Add the sugar snaps to the bowl and taste-test — add more ketjap if you fancy.
7. Serve in a deep bowl. Ready!

Jansen's pro tip

Glass noodles should naturally be gluten-free, but it's always worth checking the label!

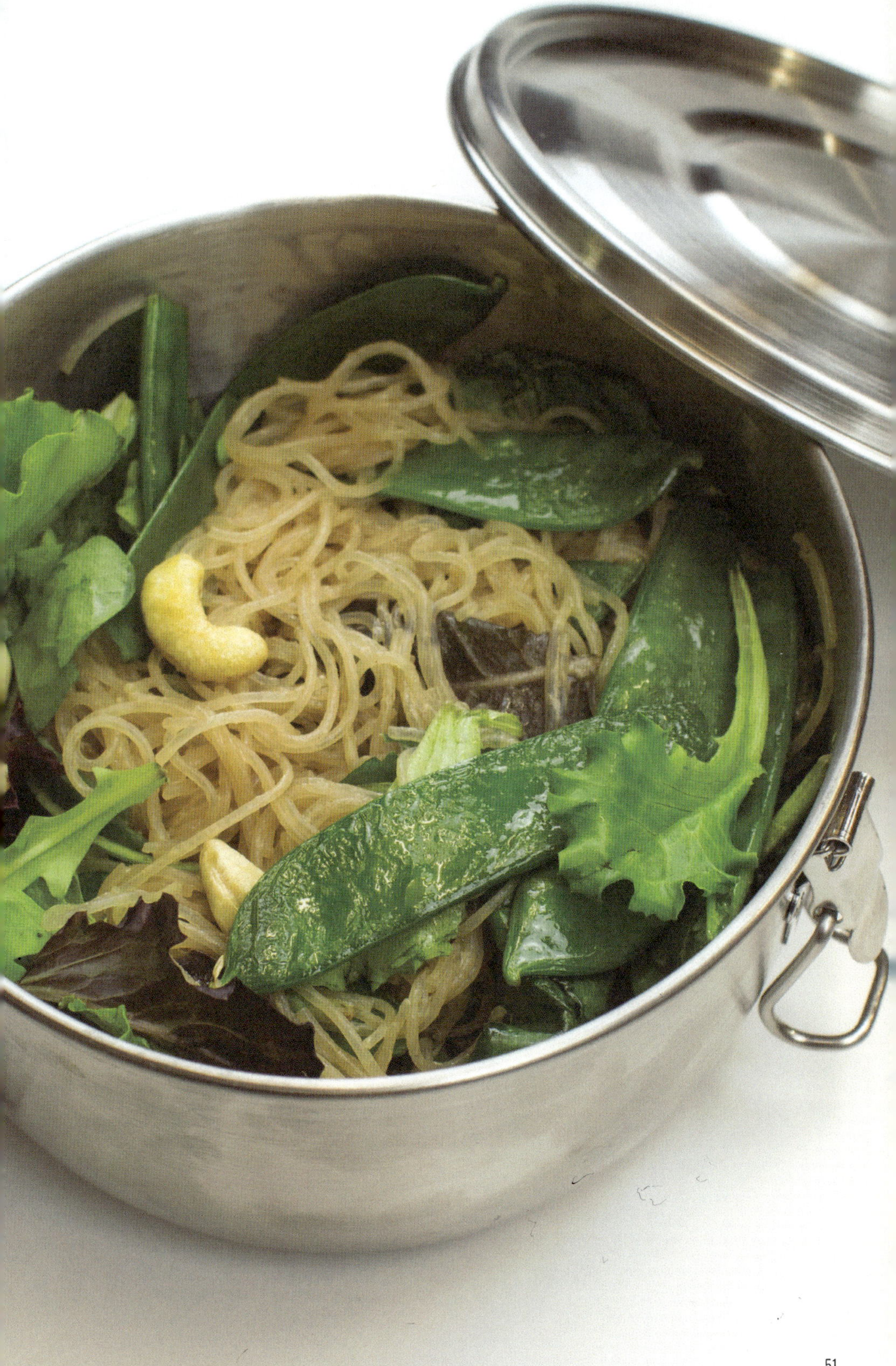

Have a Good Avo Cheddar Sandwich

Vegetarian | Vegan Option | Gluten-free Option

Servings: 2 | **Total Time:** 15 minutes
Best eaten: right away

	KCAL	FAT	CARBS	PROTEIN
Nutrition per serving:	682	48.5g	21g	15.5g

Ingredients

- 4 slices of your favourite bread (Jansen recommends Brioche bread)
- 4 slices of mature cheddar (enough to cover the bread)
- 1 avocado
- ½ small red onion
- 2 radishes
- 1 cup spinach
- Salt and pepper to taste

Instructions

1. Scoop the flesh out of the **avocado** and mash it in a bowl. Add a little **salt** and **pepper.**
2. Slice the **red onion** into really thin rings. Slice the **radish** thinly, too.
3. Give the **spinach** a quick wash.
4. In this order, place the **bread** followed by mashed avocado, spinach, **cheddar**, onion, radish, mashed avocado, bread.
5. Stick it in the oven at about 360°F/180°C and toast away! It'll take about 7–8 minutes. That's it, done!

Make it vegan

Use a vegan cheese, like cashew. There are some that taste pretty decent around now, especially when grilled. Bigger supermarkets should carry them.

Make it gluten-free

Use a gluten-free bread, many different types are now readily available. It should be easy to find in most larger supermarkets or whole food stores. Never be too shy to ask at your local bakery, either!

Jansen's pro tip

If you have a cheese toastie machine, throw it in there!

53

Green n' Lean Power Salad

Vegetarian | Gluten-free

Servings: 2 | **Total Time:** 10 minutes
Best eaten: right away, packed for lunch

Nutrition per serving:	KCAL	FAT	CARBS	PROTEIN
	485	37.5g	17g	22g

Ingredients

- 2 cups fresh green beans (2 cups = 14oz/400g)
- 1 cup frozen peas (1 cup = 7oz/200g)
- 1 ball buffalo mozzarella
- 20 leaves of basil
- 2 boiled eggs
- 6 tbsp black olives
- 2 tbsp olive oil
- Salt and pepper to taste

Instructions

1. Blanch the **green beans.** This means heat up a pot with really **salty water.** Once it's boiling like crazy throw in the beans. Cook them for about 3–5 minutes, so they don't 'squeak' anymore.
2. Throw the **peas** in for just a few seconds at the end. Then cool everything down as fast as you can. The best way to do this is to get a bowl with cold water and some ice cubes.
3. Boil the **eggs** for 6 minutes. Also cool them down and then peel the skin off when they're lukewarm.
4. Rip the **mozzarella** into pieces and halve the eggs.
5. Cut the beans roughly in half, mix in a bowl with the peas and sprinkle with a bit of **salt, pepper, olive oil.** Chop the **basil** and add that too.
6. Mix everything together, except the eggs. Serve, and finish with the eggs on top. Done!

Jansen's pro tip

Double-check the mozzarella to make sure it doesn't have animal rennet in it. There are many vegetarian varieties ('microbial' or 'vegetarian rennet') around and it always pays to check the label.

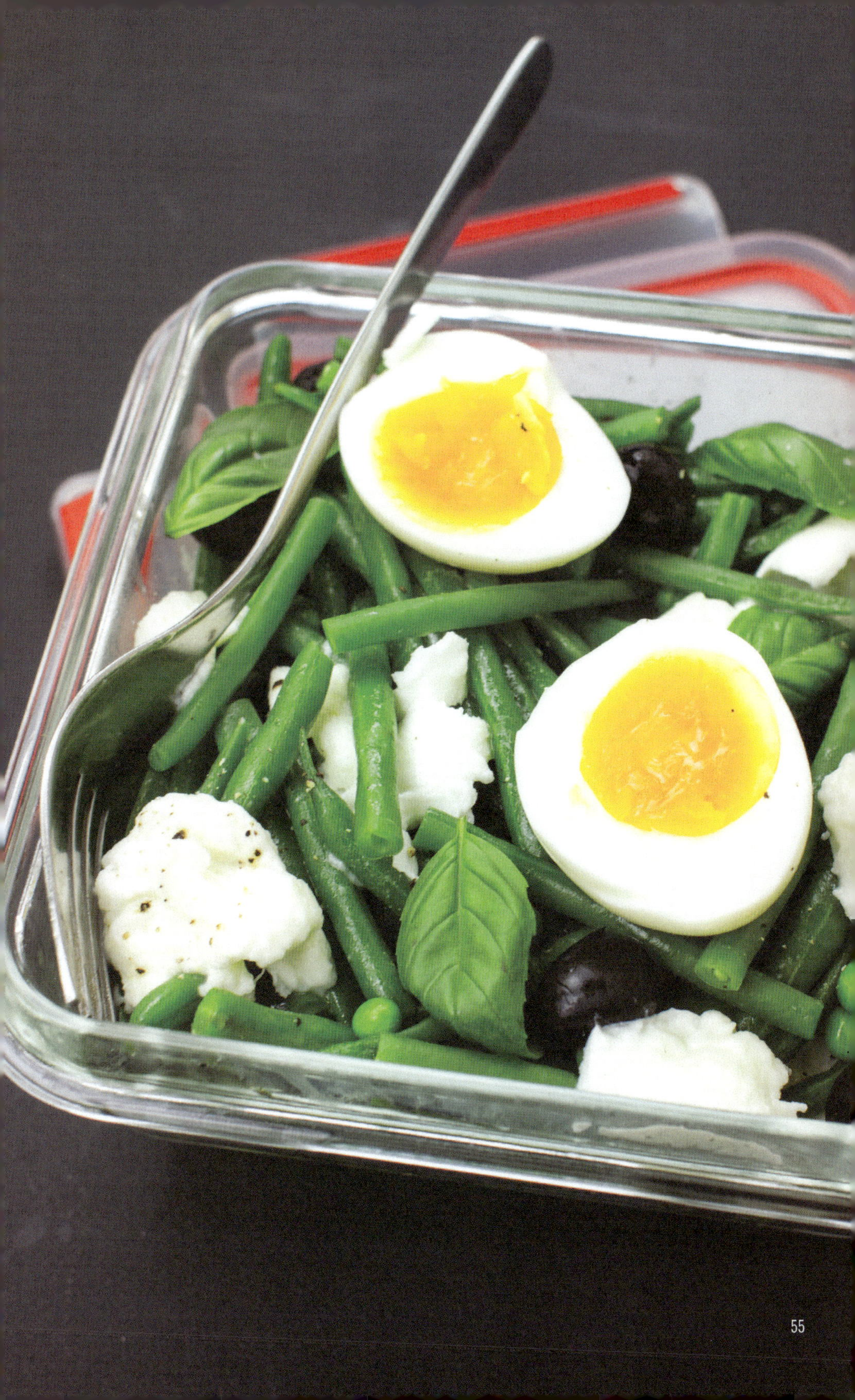

Cool Watermelon and Brash Bulgur

Vegetarian | Vegan Option | Gluten-free Option

Servings: 2 | **Total Time:** 15 minutes
Best eaten: right away, packed for lunch

Nutrition per serving:	KCAL	FAT	CARBS	PROTEIN
	360	16g	45g	13g

Ingredients

- ½ cup bulgur (½ cup = 70g)
- ⅛ watermelon (about 7oz/200g) (keep the rest for snacking!)
- 1 cup feta (1 cup = 75g)
- ½ red onion, finely diced
- 15 mint leaves
- 1 cup mixed leaf salad (1 cup = 50g)
- 2 tbsp vinegar
- 1 tsp salt
- 1 tbsp olive oil

Instructions

1. Cook the **bulgur** according to package instructions. Make sure you add a good pinch of **salt** to the water. Don't cook it tooooo dry, no worries if there's a bit of moisture left. Let it cool down.
2. Skin and cut the **watermelon** into small cubes, say 2×2cm.
3. Finely chop the **mint leaves.** Dice the **red onion,** too.
4. Put the cooled bulgur, watermelon, finely chopped mint, and red onion into a bowl. Crumble **feta** in too. Add **salt, pepper, olive oil** and **vinegar** to taste. Mix it all together well. Stack a little **mixed-leaf salad** on top so it looks pretty. Serve!

Make it vegan

Swap the feta for smoked tofu! Easy.

Make it gluten-free

Bulgur contains gluten, so you'll have to find another grain — quinoa or brown rice work well here, too!

Jansen's pro tip

Cut the watermelon and mint the night before and put it in the fridge, the watermelon will soak up all that mint so the salad is even more refreshing. Keep it all in the fridge before serving, it's at its best when cold!

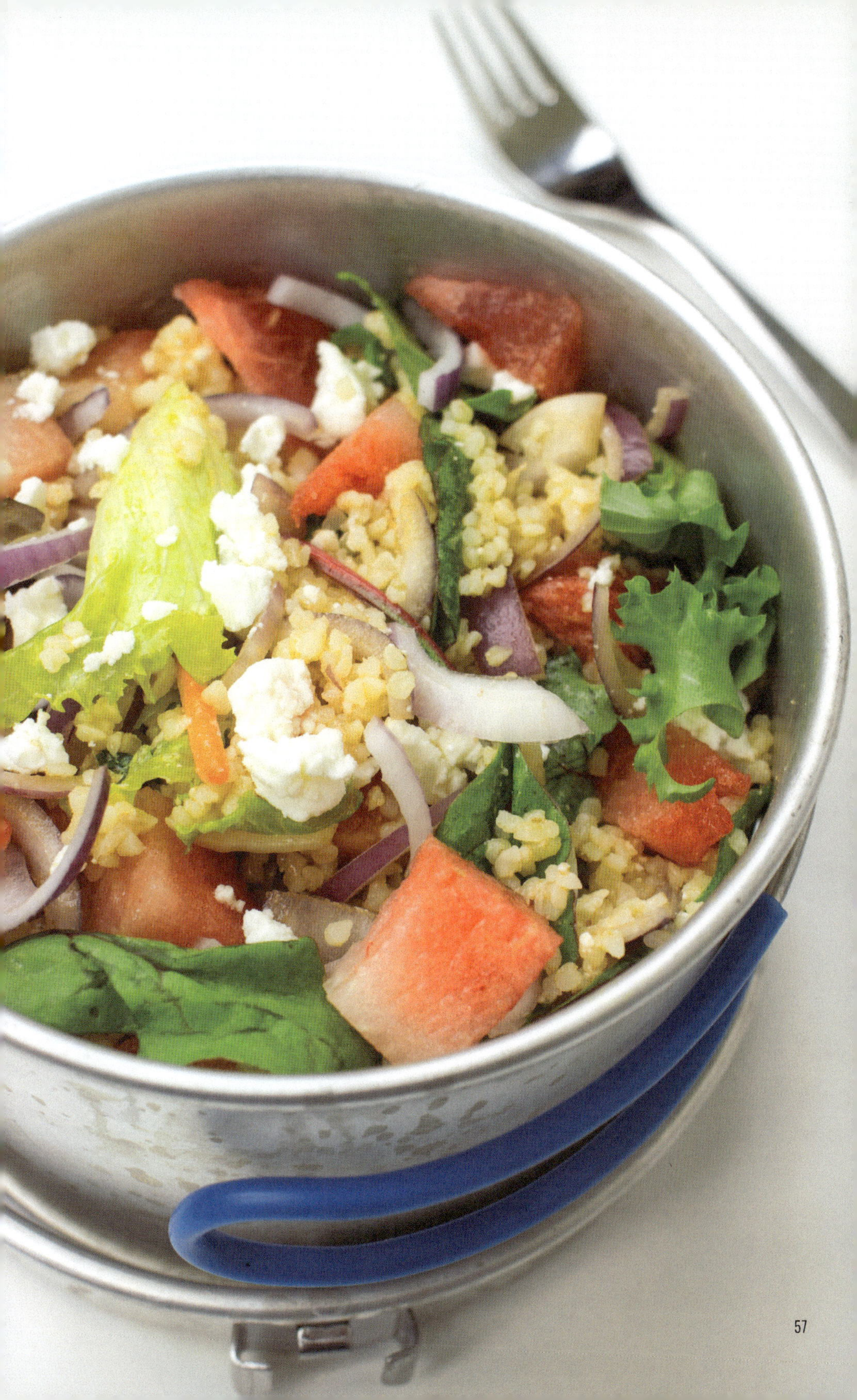

Crunchy Rostis with Green Asparagus

Vegetarian | Gluten-free

Servings: 1 | **Total Time:** 25 minutes
Best eaten: right away, packed for lunch

Nutrition per serving:	KCAL	FAT	CARBS	PROTEIN
	702	33.5g	77.5g	28g

Ingredients

- 2 medium-large potatoes
- 1 egg
- 6 slices of camembert or brie
- 6 green asparagus
- 1 tbsp olive oil
- Salt and pepper to taste

Instructions

1. Peel the **potatoes** and grate them. Add some **salt** to the grated potatoes and give them a good stir so the potatoes start to lose a bit of water. Discard the excess water.
2. Add a little more salt and some cracked black **pepper**. Add the **egg** and give the mix a good stir.
3. Heat up the **olive oil** in a pan, then pour potato-egg mix in a patty-sized shapes and fry on low to medium heat for 7 minutes on each side.
4. In another pan, fry the **asparagus** for 4 minutes so that they're still green, crunchy and yummy.
5. Assemble the rostis with the **camembert** and grilled asparagus. Enjoy!

Jansen's pro tip

Skip the eggs if you like! The egg is used as a binder here, and a 'flax egg' works perfectly well. Simply mix 1 tbsp flax seeds with 3 tbsp boiling water and stir. Let it cool for a few minutes and then use it in place of the egg. Voilà.

59

Moroccan Lentil and Feta Salad

Vegetarian | Gluten-free

Servings: 2 | **Total Time:** 30 minutes
Best eaten: right away, packed for lunch

Nutrition per serving:	KCAL	FAT	CARBS	PROTEIN
	727	41.5g	63g	27.5g

Ingredients

- ¾ cup brown lentils (¾ cup = 150g)
- 2 stalks of celery
- 3 figs
- ¾ cup feta (¾ cup = 100g)
- 2 tbsp Ras el Hanout (or curry powder)
- 2 cups baby leaf salad (2 cups = 150g) (or any mild salad)
- 4 tbsp olive oil
- 4 tbsp balsamic vinegar
- Pinch of salt

Instructions

1. Cook the **lentils** according to packet instructions until tender. Let them cool a bit, and then season with **salt, olive oil, vinegar** and **Ras el Hanout** (or **curry powder**).
2. Cut the **celery** into small cubes and add to the lentils. Crumble the **feta** in too.
3. Add the **baby leaf salad** and give it a good toss. Plate it and put the sliced **figs** on top.

Jansen's pro tip

If it's not fig season, dried ones work really well too.

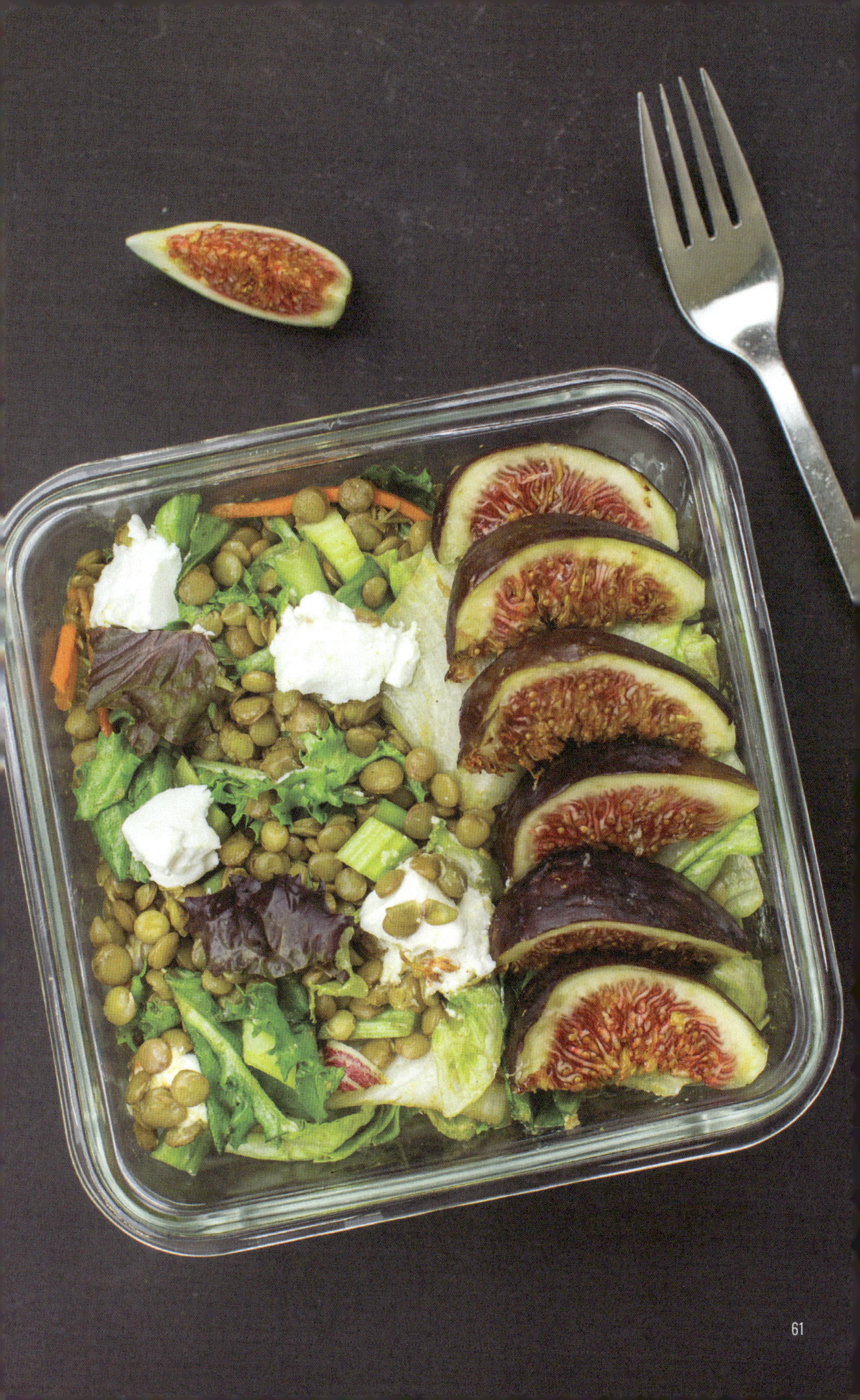

Hawaii Toast

Vegetarian | Vegan Option | Gluten-free Option

Servings: 4 | **Total Time:** 12 minutes
Best eaten: right away

Nutrition per serving:	KCAL	FAT	CARBS	PROTEIN
	347	13.5g	38.5g	17g

Ingredients
4 rustic bread slices
6 pineapple rings (from a can)
4 slices of cheddar
¾ cup smoked tofu
 (¾ cup = 200g)
4 tbsp tomato paste
Pinch of salt

Instructions
1. Spread the **tomato paste** onto the **bread.**
2. Thinly slice the **smoked tofu** and layer that on next.
3. After that is the **pineapple** — lay two rings on each bread.
4. Add the **cheese** and grill for 3–4 minutes or bake at 200°C/390°F for 6–7 minutes.
5. When browned, remove from oven and sprinkle on a little **salt** to serve. Yum!

Make it vegan
Use cashew cheese — it normally tastes better melted anyway!

Make it gluten-free
Hunt down some gluten-free bread! There's lots available from organic/whole food stores!

Jansen's pro tip
Use a garlic mayonnaise instead of tomato paste for a completely different, but equally great taste!

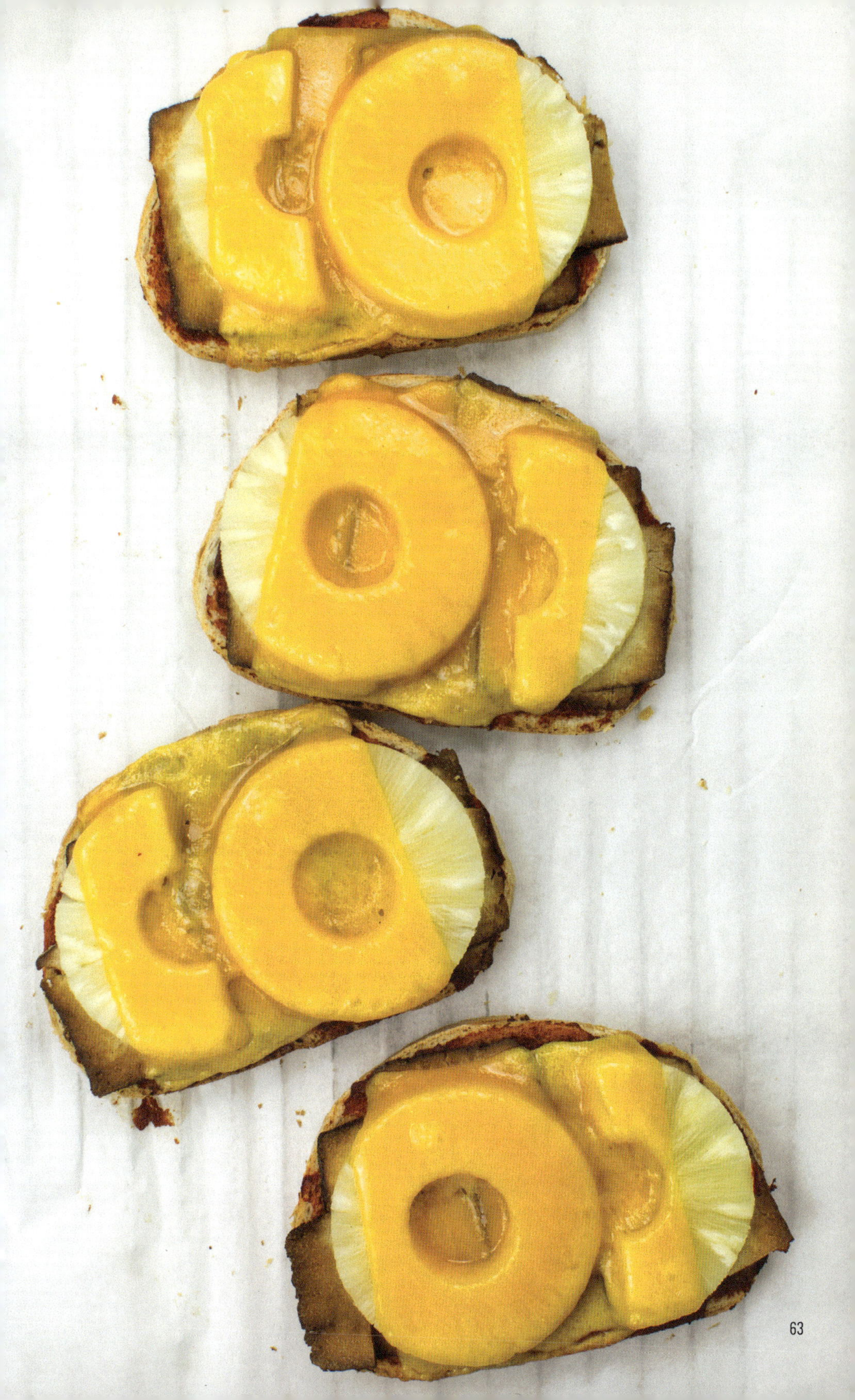

Chickpea Fritters with a Refreshing Cucumber Dip

Vegetarian | Vegan Option | Gluten-free

Servings: 2 | **Total Time:** 20 minutes
Best eaten: right away, packed for lunch

	KCAL	FAT	CARBS	PROTEIN
Nutrition per serving:	342	16g	37g	16g

Ingredients

- 1 can of chickpeas (1 can = dry weight ca. 9oz/265g)
- ¾ cucumber
- ⅗ cup yoghurt (⅗ cup = 150g)
- 1 tsp cumin
- 1 egg (or use a 'flax egg', see 'Jansen's pro tip' below)
- 1 tbsp vinegar
- 2 cups baby leaf (or favourite) salad
- 1 tbsp olive oil
- 1 tsp salt
- ½ tsp pepper

Instructions

1. Drain the **chickpeas** and give them a good rinse. Put just ¾ of them into a food processor. Add the **eggs** and 1 tbsp of **cumin.** Blend until smooth then transfer it to a bowl with the other chickpeas. Add a little **salt** and stir.
2. Heat up a non-stick frying pan on medium heat with a little **olive oil.**
3. Make the chickpea mix into small fritters and fry on each side for about 4 minutes on medium heat.
4. While frying the chickpeas, grate the **cucumber** and add **salt, pepper** and the **yoghurt.** Add a tbsp of **vinegar.**
5. Once all the fritters are done, serve them with a little salad underneath and in between and drizzle the **cucumber yoghurt** over everything.

Make it vegan
Use a vegan yoghurt (like soy) and 'flax eggs'!

Jansen's pro tip
To make a 'flax egg', simply mix 1 tbsp ground flax seeds with 3 tbsp boiling water, stir and leave to settle and cool for a couple of minutes.

65

Potato meets Beets

Vegetarian | Vegan Option | Gluten-free

Servings: 1 | **Total Time:** 25 minutes
Best eaten: right away

Nutrition per serving:	KCAL	FAT	CARBS	PROTEIN
	692	36g	84g	14.5g

Ingredients

1 beetroot, pre-cooked
⅓ cup creme fraiche (⅓ cup = 80g)
½ lime
1 tbsp olive oil
3 tbsp sunflower seeds
2 cups baby leaf salad (or another mild salad)
4 medium potatoes (roughly 14oz/400g)
Salt and pepper to taste

Instructions

1. Peel, then chop and boil the **potatoes** until soft. Zest and juice the **lime**.
2. In the meantime, mix the **creme fraiche** with the **lime zest, juice** and some **salt, pepper** and 1 tbsp of **olive oil** to make it smooth.
3. Chop the **beetroot** and put it on a plate, drizzle the creme fraiche over the beetroot, add the **baby leaf** on top, drizzle some more olive oil over it and sprinkle the **sunflower seeds** on top.
4. Gently mash the potato and serve on the side. That's it!

Make it vegan

Swap the creme fraiche for a soy yogurt or dip. Yummy!

Jansen's pro tip

If you're a 'crunch' lover, swap out the sunflower seeds for your favourite nuts, and chop them roughly. Sprinkle over the dish just before serving.

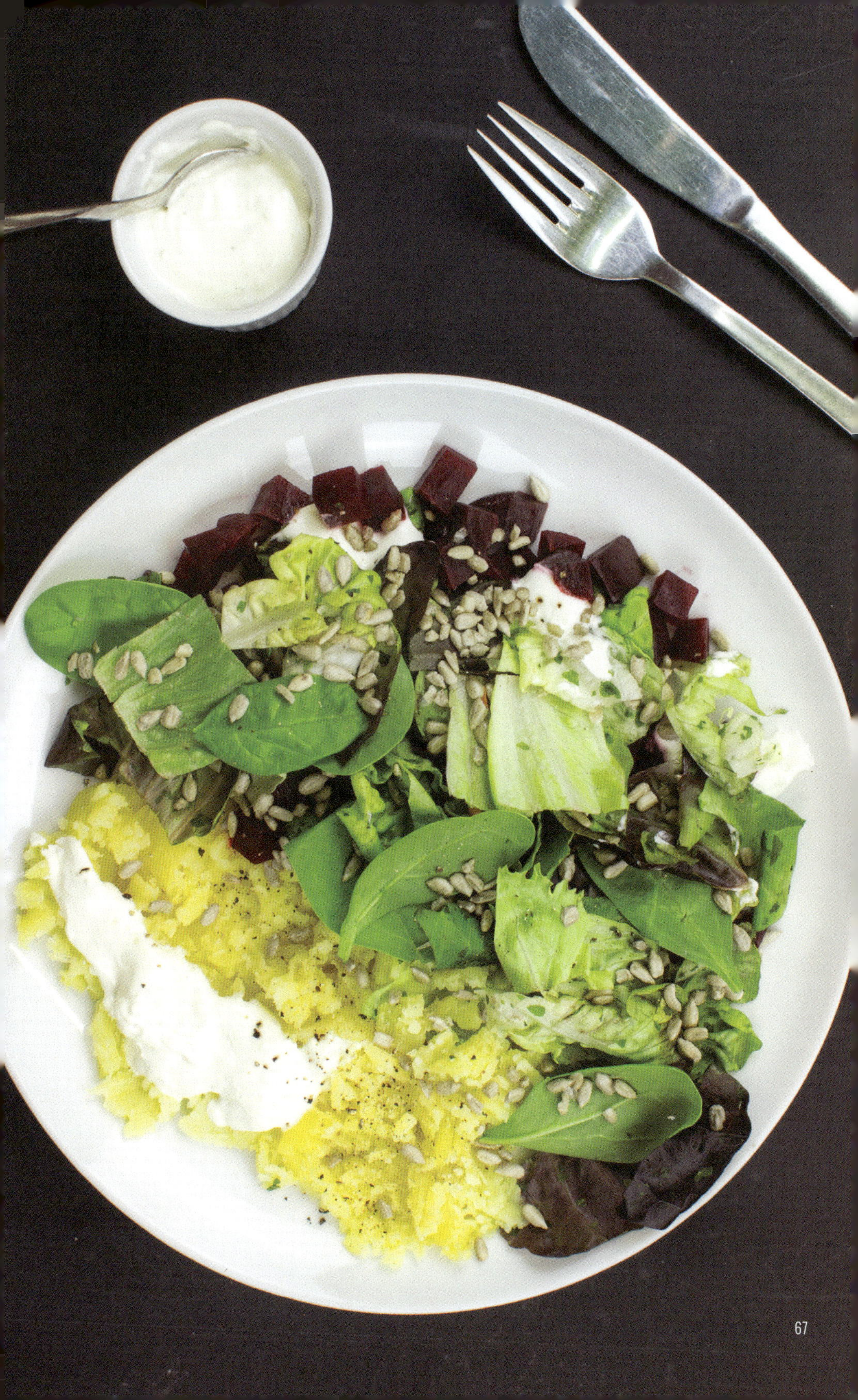

Luscious Fennel & Orange Polenta

Vegan | Gluten-free

Servings: 2 | **Total Time:** 25 minutes
Best eaten: right away, packed for lunch

Nutrition per serving:	KCAL	FAT	CARBS	PROTEIN
	455	20g	67.5g	8.5g

Ingredients

½ cup polenta
(½ cup = 100g)
1 ⅔ cup water
(1 ⅔ cup = 400ml)
2 oranges
1 fennel
1 tbsp sesame seeds
2 tbsp hazelnuts
1 cup baby spinach
2 tbsp olive oil
Salt and pepper to taste

Instructions

1. Zest the **orange,** take the **filets** out of the orange and put them in a bowl with the **zest.**
2. Squeeze as much **juice** out from the rind as possible and add it to your water cups.
3. Thinly slice the **fennel,** fry on low-medium heat with a little **olive oil** until tender but still slightly crunchy. Depending on how thinly you've sliced it, it will take just 2–3 minutes.
4. Boil the juice/water and add **salt,** stir in the **polenta** and add 2 tbsp of olive oil so it's nicely creamy. Cook for about 5 minutes. Then add the orange filets and **pepper** and stir them in gently.
5. While that's happening, give the **hazelnuts** a quick chop and toast them in a pan with the **sesame seeds.**
6. Stir the fennel and **spinach** into the polenta. Serve in a bowl and garnish with the toasted sesame seeds and hazelnuts.

Jansen's pro tip
Delicious hot or cold, perfect for packing for lunch!

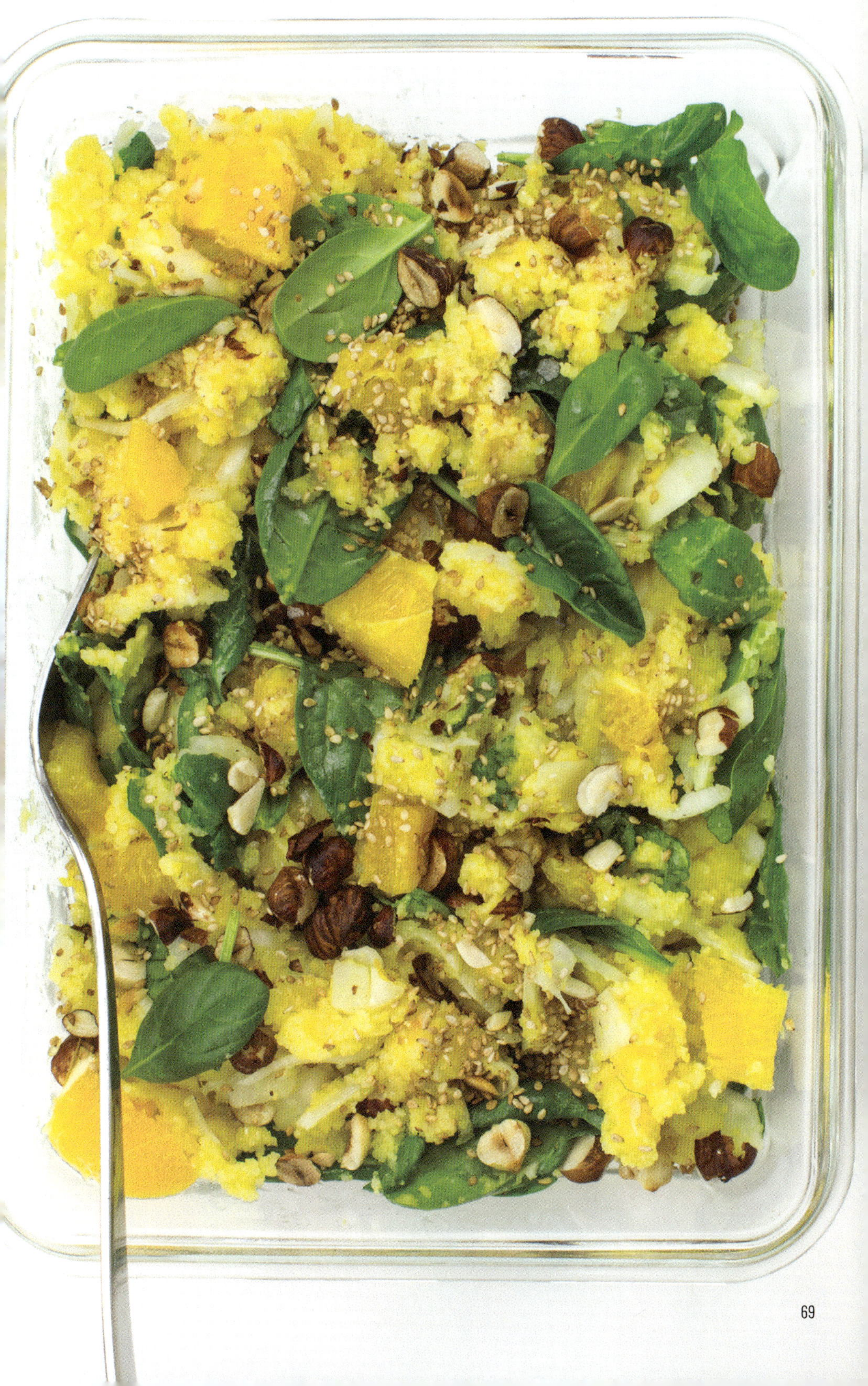

Disclaimer

Great care has been taken to provide accurate nutritional information with each recipe. However, please note it is for guideline purposes only and we make no guarantee as to the accuracy of this information. Please consult a doctor before making any decisions about treatment of any conditions you may have, or think you may have.

Thanks

**FOR READING,
AND AS ALWAYS THANKS
FOR YOUR SUPPORT.**

Enjoy lunch!

Annex

1. Vegan, GF Option — Creamy Mushroom Penne — 6 ingredients, 20 minutes, 17.5g protein per serving (543 kcal), 12.9g protein on 400 kcal

2. Vegetarian, Gluten-free — Celerybration Salad — 6 ingredients, 10 minutes, 16g protein per serving (374 kcal), 17g protein on 400 kcal

3. Vegan, Gluten-free, — Cranberry and Orange Sweet Potato Salad, 5 ingredients, 15 minutes, 4g protein per serving (252 kcal), 6.4g protein on 400 kcal

4. Vegetarian, GF Option — Golden Leek and Pear Puff Pastry, 30 minutes, 7g protein per serving (300 kcal), 9.5g protein on 400 kcal

5. Vegetarian, Vegan Option, Gluten-free — Chickpea Tacos with Chargrilled Peppers, 10g protein per serving (542 kcal), 7.5g protein on 400 kcal

6. Vegan, Gluten-free — Avocado Chia Smoothie Bowl, 6 ingredients, 3 minutes, 5g protein per serving (374 kcal), 5.5g protein on 400 kcal

7. Vegan, Gluten-free — Oven-baked Mega Mash, 6 ingredients, 30 minutes, 15g protein per serving (768 kcal), 8g protein on 400 kcal

8. Vegan, Gluten-free — Sweet Roast Pumpkin with Rocket Pesto, 6 ingredients, 30 minutes, 16g protein per serving (772 kcal), 8.5g protein on 400 kcal

9. Vegan, GF Option — Gnocchi Balboa, 6 ingredients, 20 minutes, 15.5g protein per serving (711 kcal), 9g protein on 400 kcal

10. Vegan, Gluten-free — Saucy Oven Carrots with Smoky Tofu, 6 ingredients, 30 minutes, 18g protein per serving (432 kcal), 16.5g protein on 400 kcal

11. Vegan, GF Option — Asian-style Hoisin and Ginger Spaghetti, 6 ingredients, 20 minutes, 18g protein per serving (580 kcal), 12.5g protein on 400 kcal

12. Vegan, Gluten-free — Raunchy Sweet Potato Salad, 6 ingredients, 30 minutes, 15g protein per serving (663 kcal), 9g protein on 400 kcal

13. Vegan, GF Option — Speedy Chickpea Stew, 6 ingredients, 20 minutes, 16g protein per serving (375 kcal), 17g protein on 400 kcal

14. Vegetarian, GF Option — Ricotta and Mushroom Empanadas, 6 ingredients, 30 minutes, 3g protein per serving (168 kcal), 7g protein on 400 kcal

15. Vegan, Gluten-free — Crispy Potato Medley, 6 ingredients, 30 minutes, 11.5g protein per serving (439 kcal), 10.5g protein on 400 kcal

16. Vegetarian, GF Option — Royal Quesadillas // Kat: 6 ingredients, 25 minutes, 21g protein per serving (618 kcal), 13.5g protein on 400 kcal // Sofia: 6 ingredients, 25 minutes, 22g per serving (655 kcal), 13.5g protein on 400 kcal

17. Vegan, Gluten-free — Crunchy Fennel and Grapefruit Salad, 5 ingredients, 10 minutes, 7g protein per serving (340 kcal), 8.5g protein on 400 kcal

18. Vegetarian, GF Option — Melted Goat's Cheese with Honey and Pesto, 6 ingredients, 10 minutes, 8.5g protein per serving (235 kcal), 14.5g protein on 400 kcal

19. Vegetarian, Vegan Option, GF Option — ¡Ay, caramba! Sweet Potato Salad, 6 ingredients, 30 minutes, 16.5g protein per serving (619 kcal), 10.5g protein on 400 kcal

20. Vegetarian, Vegan Option — Italian Mozzarella Salad with Garlicky Croutons, 6 ingredients, 10 minutes, 16g protein per serving (493 kcal), 13g protein on 400 kcal

21. Vegan, Gluten-free — Glass Noodles in Sweet Peanut Sauce, 6 ingredients, 10 minutes, 12.5g protein per serving (413 kcal), 12g protein on 400 kcal

22. Vegetarian, Vegan Option, GF Option — Have a Good Avo Cheddar Sandwich, 6 ingredients, 15 minutes, 15.5g protein per serving (682 kcal), 9g protein on 400 kcal

23. Vegetarian, Gluten-free — Green n' Lean Power Salad, 6 ingredients, 10 minutes, 22g protein per serving (485 kcal), 18g protein on 400 kcal

24. Vegetarian, Vegan Option, GF Option — Cool Watermelon and Brash Bulgur, 6 ingredients, 15 minutes, 13g protein per serving (360 kcal), 14.5g protein on 400 kcal

25. Vegetarian, Gluten-free — Crunchy Rostis with Green Asparagus, 4 ingredients, 25 minutes, 28g protein per serving (702 kcal), 16g protein on 400 kcal

26. Vegetarian, Gluten-free — Moroccan Lentil and Feta Salad, 6 ingredients, 30 minutes, 27.5g protein per serving (727 kcal), 15g protein on 400 kcal

27. Vegetarian, Vegan Option, GF Option — Hawaii Toast, 5 ingredients, 12 minutes, 17g protein per serving (347 kcal), 19.5g protein on 400 kcal

28. Vegetarian, Vegan Option, Gluten-free — Chickpea Fritters with a Refreshing Cucumber Dip, 16g protein per serving (342 kcal), 18.5g protein on 400 kcal

29. Vegetarian, Vegan Option, Gluten-free, — Potato meets Beets, 6 ingredients, 20 minutes, 14.5g protein per serving (692 kcal), 8.5g protein on 400 kcal

30. Vegan, Gluten-free — Luscious Fennel & Orange Polenta, 6 ingredients, 25 minutes 8.5g protein per serving (455 kcal), 7.5g protein on 400 kcal

LUNCH IN *Six*

Printed in Great Britain
by Amazon